THE
ULTIMATE
ANGEL
BOOK

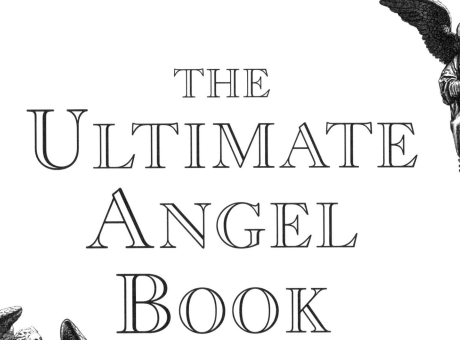

THE
ULTIMATE
ANGEL
BOOK

MORE THAN 600 CLIP ART IMAGES

COMPILED BY JIM HARTER

GRAMERCY BOOKS

NEW YORK • AVENEL

This book is dedicated
with much love
to my sisters
Marty Marmaduke
and
Barbara Harter Whitton

Introduction and Compilation copyright © 1995 by Jim Harter
All rights reserved

This edition is published by Gramercy Books,
distributed by Random House Value Publishing, Inc.
40 Engelhard Avenue, Avenel, New Jersey 07001

Production supervised by Michael Siebert
Designed by Melissa Campbell

Random House
New York • Toronto • London • Sydney • Auckland

Printed and bound in the United States of America

Library of Congress Cataloging–in–Publication Data
The ultimate angel book / edited by Jim Harter.
p. cm.
ISBN 0–517–14806–4
1. Angels in art—Miscellanea.
2. Decoration and ornament. 3. Clip art.
I. Harter, Jim.
NK1590.A53U45 1995
741.6—dc20   95–30421
                                          CIP

8 7 6 5 4 3 2 1

CONTENTS

INTRODUCTION

This is a book for everyone who loves angels. In addition, it is a definitive source of quality copyright-free images for artists, graphic designers, and desktop publishers. A collection of more than six hundred pieces of line art, it includes angels for every possible project and occasion: Christmas and Easter angels, cupids and cherubs, enchanting sentimental angels, musical angels, biblical angels, angels from other cultures, angels from Christian antiquity and from the tradition of classical western painting, angels used in nineteenth-century graphic art, on coins, furniture, monuments, and art objects, together with sculpted angels and angels carved of wood. All this and more are here in *The Ultimate Angel Book*.

Many of the engravings come from rare books and periodicals that were originally published in the United States, Germany, France, and England between 1848 and early in the twentieth century. Most of the material, however, was published during the "golden age" of wood engravings that lasted for only twenty years—from about 1870 to 1890. Angels were extremely popular in Victorian illustration and appeared regularly in such publications as *Harper's Weekly*, *Harper's Monthly*, *Frank Leslie's Monthly*, *The Aldine*, *Die Gartenlaube*, *Ueber Land und Meer*, *Moderne Kunst*, *The Illustrated London News*, *The Art Journal*, and *Journal Illustrée*. It is from these periodicals that I took many of the illustrations. Other images I culled from illustrated German books on the work of Goethe and Heinrich Heine, popular religious periodicals (mainly from England) and Bible histories, and from large, beautiful editions of the Bible, John Bunyan's *Paradise Lost*, and Dante's *Purgatorio* and *Paradiso* illustrated by Gustave Doré.

Only one of my source books focused on artistic traditions as they relate to angels. This book, *Sacred and Legendary Art* by a Mrs. Jameson, first appeared in 1848 (and was reprinted by Longmans, Green and Co., London and New York). It has a lengthy, but interesting text about angels in art, beginning with pre-Christian antiquity and ending with William Blake, and many excellent illustrations, most of which I have included in this volume.

When compiling this book my aim was to organize the material according to its popular appeal and probable usefulness as clip art. There are many images that might fit into several categories. In these cases I have placed them where they are visually most effective.

The book begins with a collection of cupids and cherubs, useful for St. Valentine's Day projects or for any that relate to love. The next section features musical angels—who are singing or playing one of a variety of musical instruments. Following this is a collection of sculpted angels, including bas reliefs, wood carvings, and art objects, and several depictions of the Arc of the Covenant.

Although angels are usually considered to be within the Judeo-Christian tradition, they were certainly known in other cultures. In Mrs. Jameson's book there are illustrations from ancient Egypt and Assyria. From other sources I found Greco-Roman winged figures. Some of these are winged versions of such popular deities as Jupiter, Saturn, Mercury, and Diana. Others, like Nike and Eros, are always depicted with wings. These images are in the section Pre-Christian Angels.

The section that follows shows angels in early Christian iconography, traditional western painting, and pre-nineteenth-century graphic art. There are a few examples of winged symbols of the four evangelists—the bull, lion, bird, and man. There is also an image of the mysterious tetramorph, a winged figure that incorporates the four evangelists. Among the engravings of classical western paintings are works by Fra Angelico, Taddeo di Bartolo, Sandro Botticelli, Jan Van Eyck, Raphael, and Albrecht Dürer.

Gustave Doré is justifiably famous for his renderings of angels. The final section has a selection of his engravings of good and bad angels—his illustrations for the Bible, Bunyan's *Paradise Lost*, and Dante's *Purgatorio* and *Paradiso*. I consider the images I have chosen to represent his best work.

Besides the roles angels play in the realm of heaven, they represent to most of us the human emotions that are the most loving, essential, pure, beautiful, creative, noble, and divine. It is no surprise, therefore, that angels maintain their enormous popularity, particularly in art of all kinds. I hope this book will be useful to you and will add to your knowledge of these heavenly creatures.

JIM HARTER

San Antonio, Texas
1995

 CUPIDS AND CHERUBS

12

13

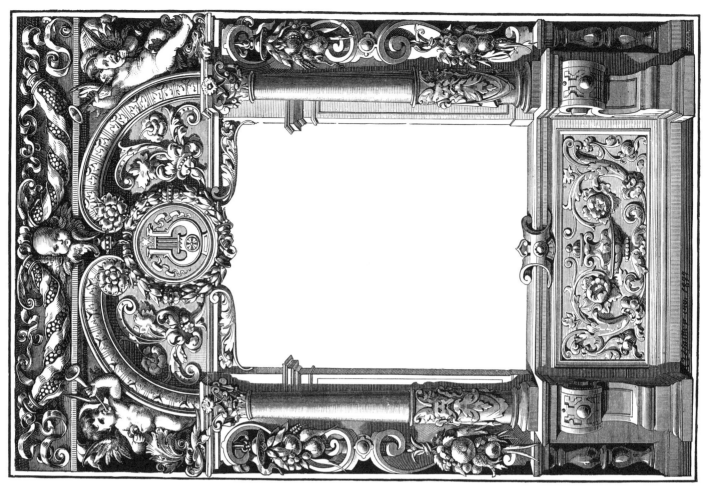

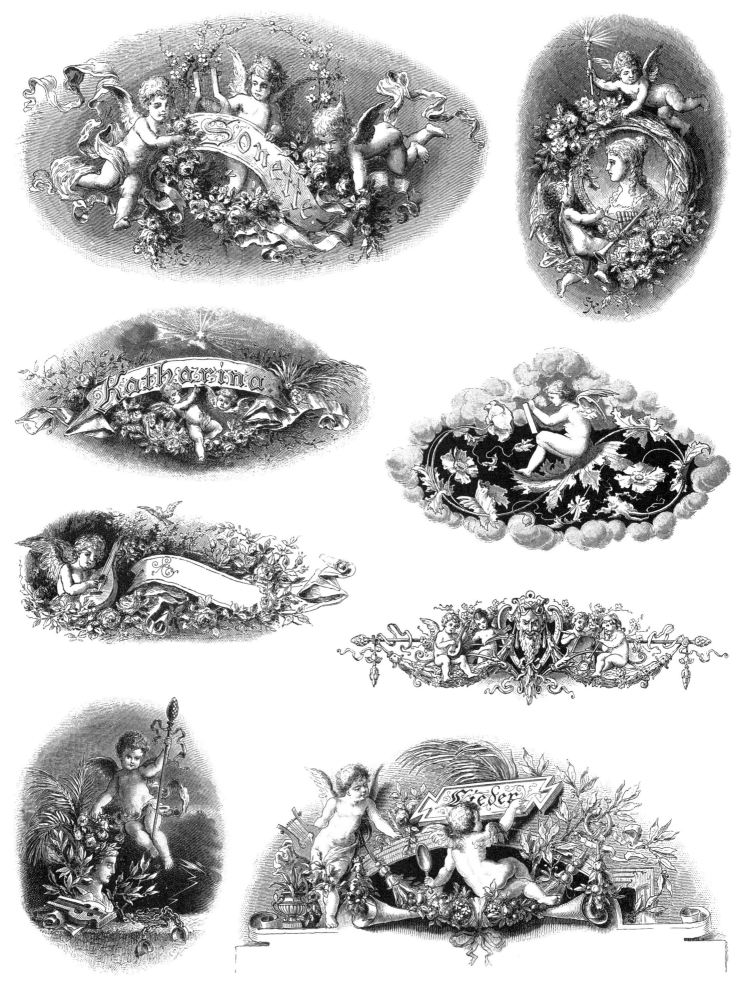

THE END

MUSICAL ANGELS

Dichterstimmen aus der Gegenwart

gesammelt

von

Friedrich Bodenstedt.

H. Götz

SCULPTED ANGELS

43

44

IN MEMORY
OF OUR
SOLDIERS AND SAILORS
WHO,
ON LAND OR AT SEA,
HAVE FALLEN
MARTYRS
FOR
LIBERTY AND LAW.
―――
PEACE
BE WITH THEM.
AMEN.

47

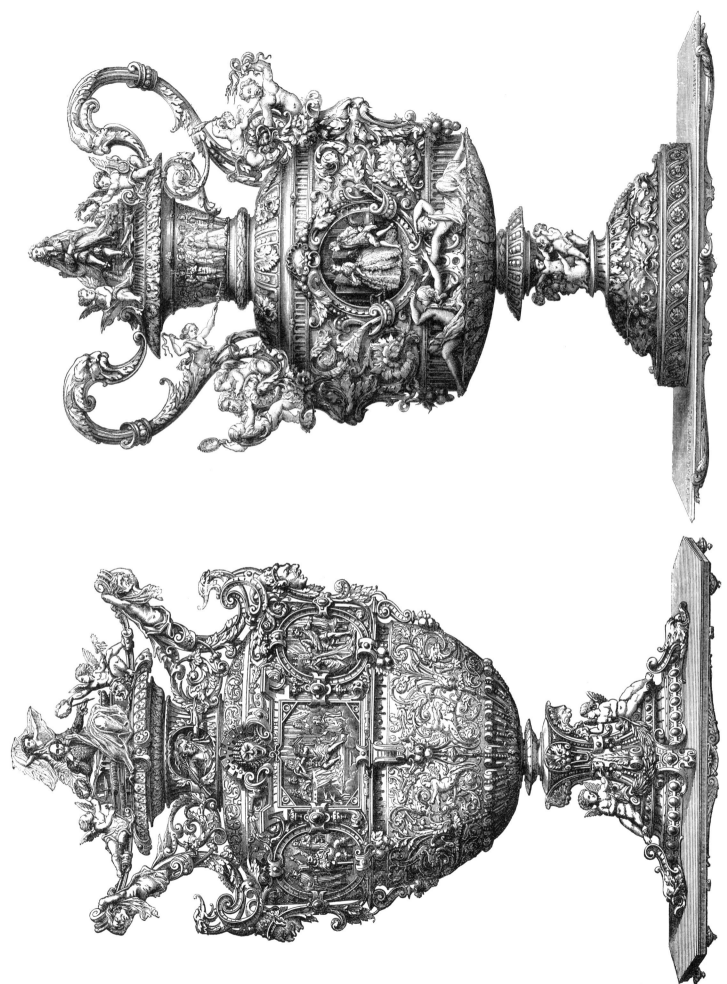

PRE-CHRISTIAN ANGELS

EPIS

NIKE

HIΠΠON ·ΛΛOS

ΘESEO

ΛBOPΛS

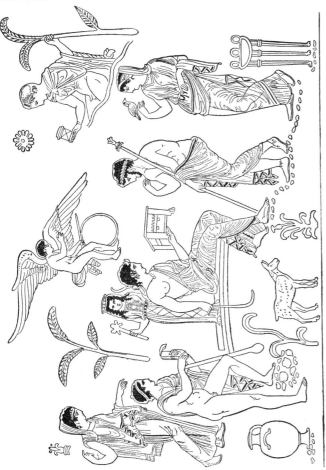

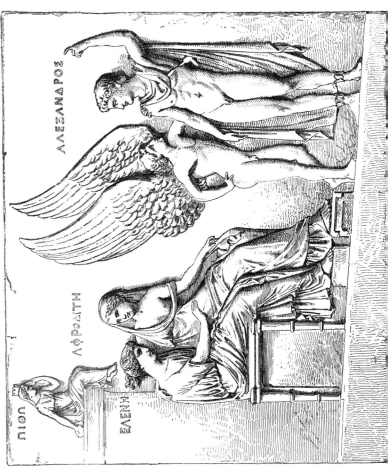

Angels in Early Christian Iconography, Classical Western Painting, and Early Graphic Art

МН СЕЦЬ

71

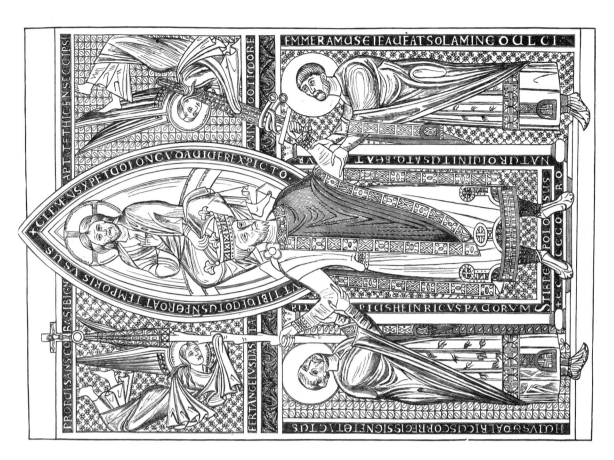

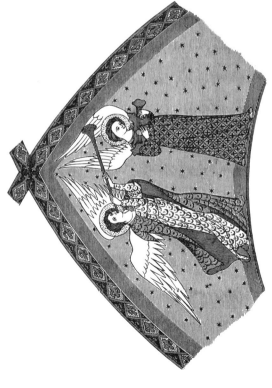

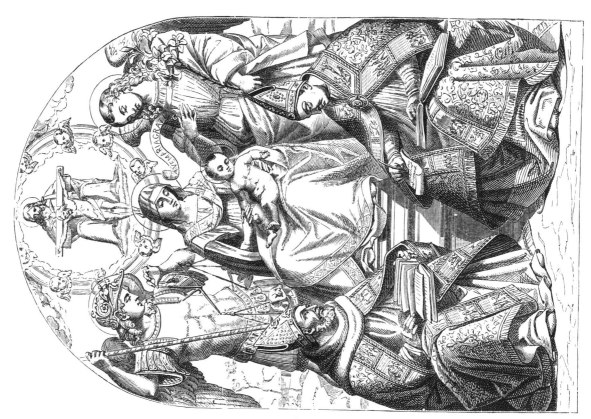

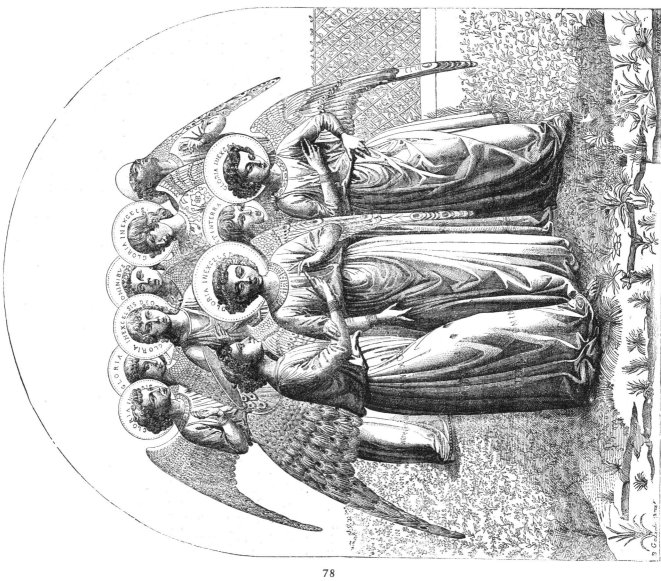

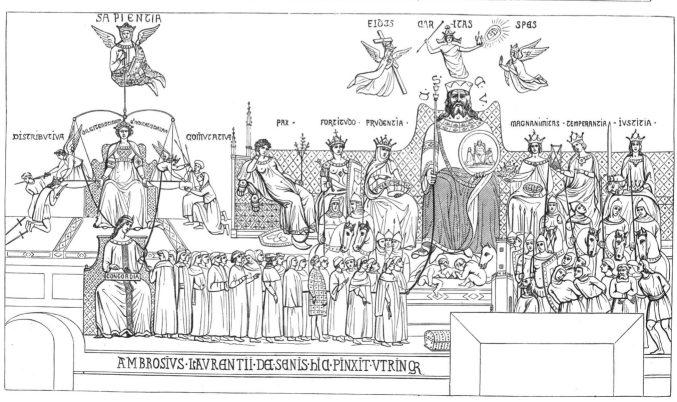

AMBROSIVS·LAVRENTII·DE·SENIS·HIC·PINXIT·VTRINQR

AVE MARIA GRATIA PLENA DOMINUS TECUM BENEDICTA TU

Ra: Vrbinas inu.

Mercurius

Inter Venerem et Lunam apparet. Domus ejus principalis Virgo, minus principalis Gemini.

Ra: Vrbinas inu.

Eq.s N.ᵗ Dorigny del: & sculp.

Sol

Planetarum medius et maximus. Domus ejus Leo

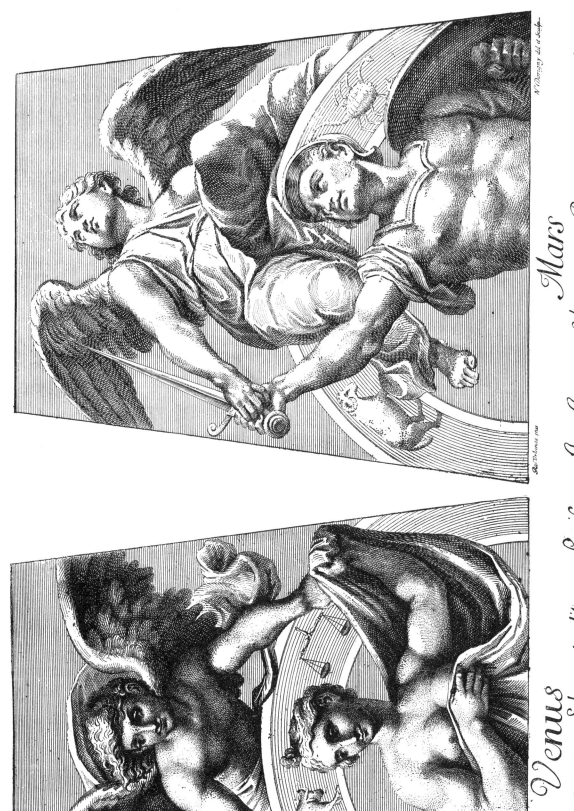

Raf. Urbinas jnv:

Venus

Planeta est soli proximus, cum Solem antecedit mane Lucifer
quasi lucem ferens; cumq; eundem sequitur Vesperi Hesperus

Raf Urbinas inu

Mars

Inter Jovem et Solem apparet. Domus eius principalis
Scorpius, minus principalis Aries,

N. Dorigny del et Sculp.

94

Rex Vrbinas inu.

N. Dorigny del. et Sculp.

Jupiter

Saturno proximus. Domus ejus principalis Sagittarius,
minus principalis Pisces.

Saturnus

Omnium Planetarum supremus. Domus ejus principalis
Aquarius, minus principalis Capricornus.

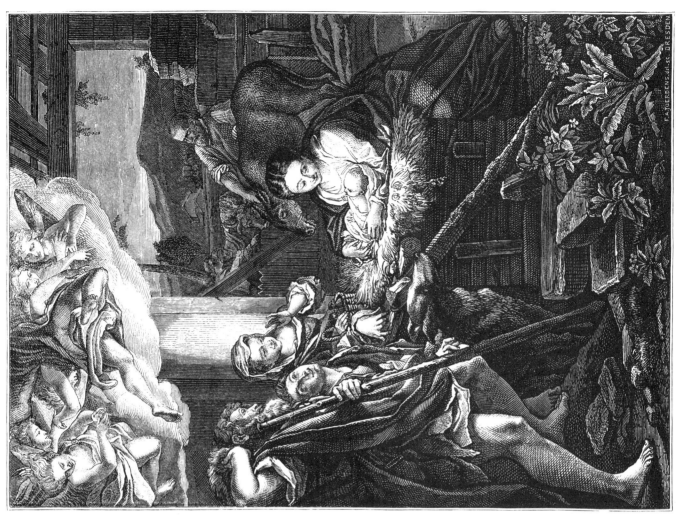

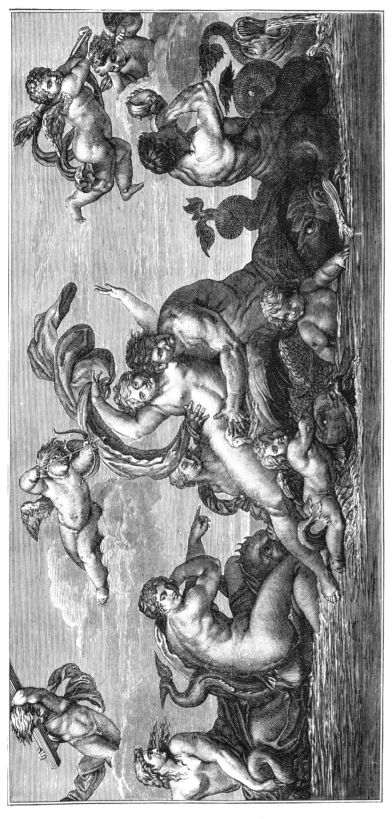

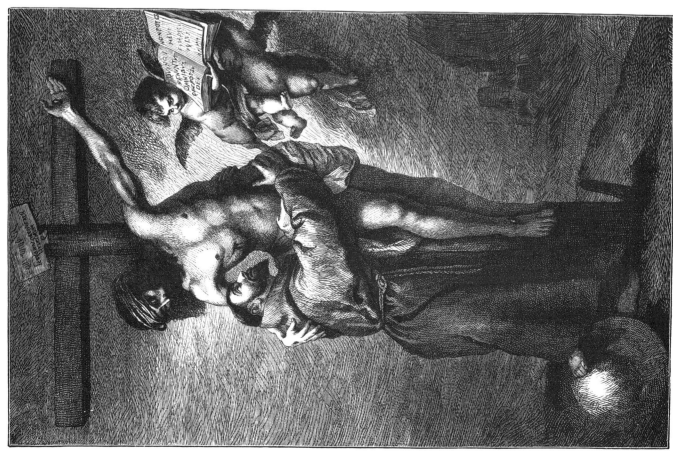

Biblia/ das ist/ die gantze Heilige Schrifft Deudsch.

Mart. Luth.

Wittemberg.

Begnadet mit Kür=
furstlicher zu Sachsen
freiheit.

Gedruckt durch Hans Lufft.

M. D. XXXIIII.

IOANNI V
LVSIT ET ALGARB
REGI
SCIENTIAE ARTESQVE
AVCTAE AC DITATAE

224
1120

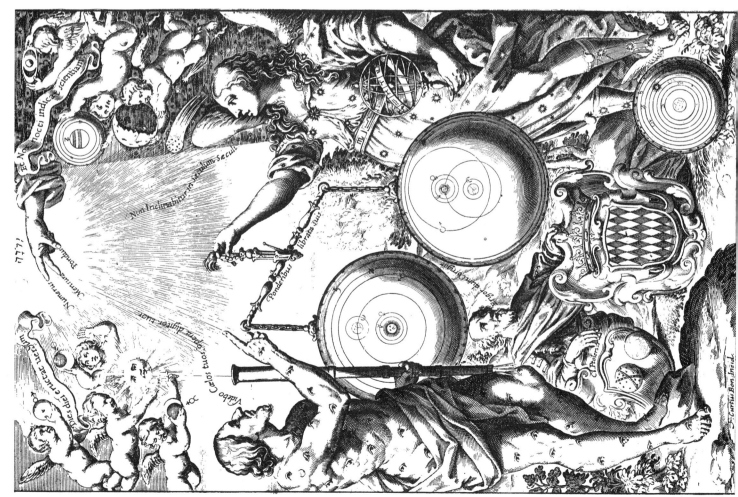

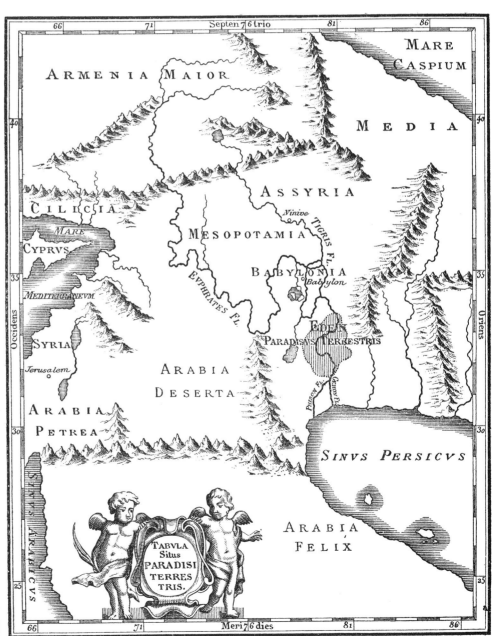

TABVLA
Situs
PARADISI
TERRES
TRIS.

VALEN FLOREAS
TINE IN DEO

VALENTINE
VALENTINE VALENTINE
VIVAS LEGE VIVAS
FLOREAS GAVDEAS
FELICITER

FVRIVS
DIONV
SIVS

FILIOC
LVSTIT
LAVIT

Gravé par E. Morieu r. Vavin 45 Paris.

109

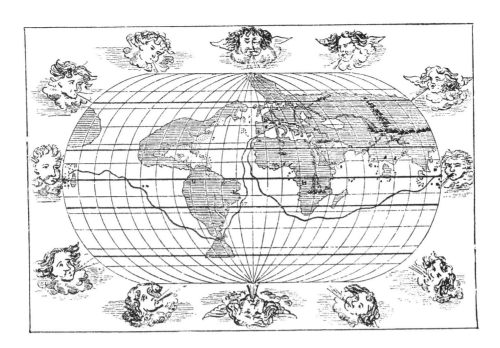

Angels in
Nineteenth-Century
Graphic Art

F. Weslig.

THROUGH A GLASS DARKLY

BY ELLEN·M·H·GATES

How many times, within the glass,
I see a figure pause and pass;
As like myself as it can be,
And yet it scarcely looks at me.

But one day, one, before the glass
I paused, and did not dare to pass;
For there, with some foreknowledge lit,
A face looked out—I looked at it.

The sad eyes pierced me through and through,
From the set lips a challenge flew;
As it had passed through searching flame,
A voice, imperious, called my name.

Before some clear, inshining light,
My earthly atoms fled from sight;
As that which evermore would be,
My soul itself confronted me.

I looked at it, ashamed, dismayed;
It wore a crown—I was afraid;
As one who might, it made demands
Of blood and brain, of heart and hands.

It questioned me, it whispered clear
Great secrets that I ought to hear;
It bade me keep, in solemn trust,
Its royal purple from the dust.

The tryst was ended—I could see
A veil drop down 'twixt it and me;
I had no question more to ask
Of Life or Death—I knew my task.

133

141

142

"Behold, I am alive forevermore."

II. Religion und Philosophie.

148

AACHEN

WORMS

SPEYER

149

ANIMA·MVNDVS DEVS.

VON

KANT

BIS

HEGEL.

151

Die Malzheser

Der Neffe als Onkel.

Lustspiel in drei Aufzügen
Aus dem Französischen
des Picard.

Wilhelm Tell.

Schauspiel.

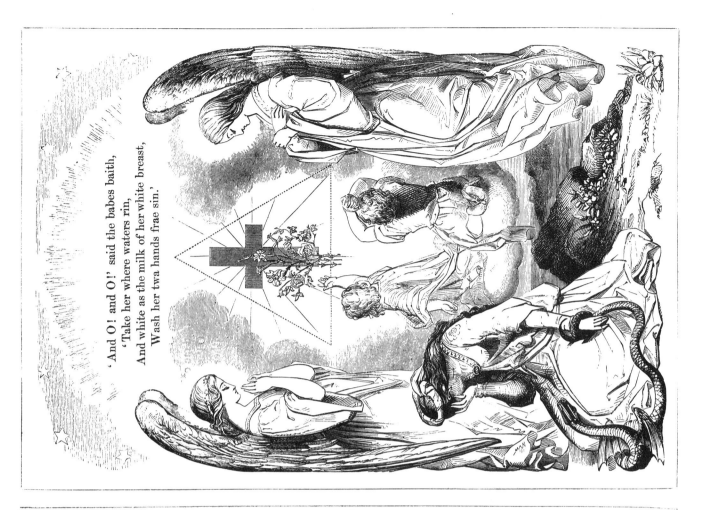

'And O! and O!' said the babes baith,
  'Take her where waters rin,
And white as the milk of her white breast,
  Wash her twa hands frae sin.'

Rudiger.

"Now help me, Jesus!" loud she cries,
  And loud on God she calls ;
Then from the grasp of Rudiger
  The little infant falls.

And loud he shriek'd, for now his frame
  The huge black arms clasp'd round,
And dragg'd the wretched Rudiger
  Adown the dark profound.

WHEEL OF TIME.

1854.

Angels in Nineteenth-Century Biblical Illustration

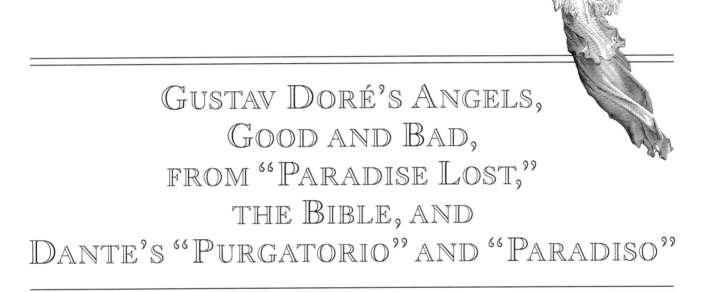

Gustav Doré's Angels,
Good and Bad,
from "Paradise Lost,"
the Bible, and
Dante's "Purgatorio" and "Paradiso"

186

207